WONDERFUL
WILD

ANIMALS

Illustrated by Greg and Tim Hildebrandt

Adapted from the original text by Simone Zapun

PUBLISHERS · GROSSET & DUNLAP · NEW YORK

Copyright © 1989, 1979 by Platt & Munk, Publishers,
a division of Grosset & Dunlap, Inc., a member of
The Putnam Publishing Group, New York.
All rights reserved.
Published simultaneously in Canada. Printed in Singapore.
Library of Congress Catalog Card Number: 88-81712
ISBN 0-448-09078-3   A B C D E F G H I J

Previously published as *Games Animals Play*.

 # Table of Contents

Baby Riders

As soon as certain baby animals are born, they go for rides with their mothers. Wherever the mothers go, the babies go. Whatever the mothers hear, see, and smell, the babies do, too. But different baby animals ride in different ways. Some sit on their mothers' backs, others cling to their mothers' fur, and still others snuggle in the pouches of their mothers' stomachs.

Swans

High over little farmhouses in the South American Andes, Mother Black-Necked Swan flies with her babies on her back. Slowly, she glides down to a pond where there are lots of waterlilies. Here she floats while her babies nap between her wings. As soon as they awaken, the babies jump in the water to swim all by themselves. But Mother Swan keeps a watchful eye on them.

Koala Bears

When a baby koala is born, it is tiny—only one inch long. After birth it climbs into its mother's pouch—a pocket on her stomach—and there it rides and grows. After six months, the baby koala is too big to fit inside the pouch. It climbs out of the pouch and onto the mother's back where it rides piggyback until it is one year old. By then the baby is almost as big as its mother—two feet high and nice and plump.

Sloths

The three-toed sloth always seems to be napping. With its claws wrapped around tree branches, it hangs upside down like a swinging hammock. Actually, the sloth is very much awake. It would rather spend time slowly traveling from branch to branch than walking about on the ground. A baby sloth travels by grabbing onto the thick fur of its mother's underbelly and swinging along with her. When the mother sloth is hungry, she holds her baby in her arms and chews on tender leaves.

Kangaroos

Mother Kangaroo hops over the Australian grasslands carrying her baby in her pouch. When the baby was first born it crawled into the pouch of skin on its mother's stomach. At the time it was so small that it didn't even look like a kangaroo. It looked more like a tiny, fat worm. Now, after about six months, it is a gangly little roo, almost too big for the pouch. This playful baby is called a joey. It can grab blades of grass and nibble on leaves. Sometimes it even jumps in and out of its mother's pouch.

Giant Anteaters

Mother Anteater shuffles through swamps and forests without fear of losing her baby. The baby clings to its mother's shaggy gray-brown fur and rides on her back. If the baby slips, it will not fall far. It will grab hold of the mother's long bushy tail. From time to time, Mother Anteater pokes her long nose into ant and termite nests. With her sticky tongue, she is able to pop the insects into her mouth. And she pops a few snacks into her baby's mouth, too.

Amazing Tails

Since people don't have tails, it is hard for us to know how helpful and how much fun they can be. But animals know. Animals use their tails to hang from branches, swim and run, carry twigs, hold their babies, keep themselves warm, and show their beauty.

Opossums

The opossum's long, thin tail is handy for many important duties. A mother opossum carries her newborn babies in her pouch. After ten weeks they climb out and ride on her back. The mother opossum wraps her tail around the babies like a wire coat hanger so they will not topple off.

When an opossum builds a home, it hooks its tail around leaves and twigs and carries them to a log where it makes a nest.

To eat, an opossum just winds its tail around a branch, swings down, and picks a piece of the juicy fruit hanging there.

Muskrats

Muskrats are champion swimmers. They quietly dive into ponds and stay underwater for up to 17 minutes. When they come up for air, they dog paddle backwards and forwards. Why are they such good swimmers? Because they use their long, narrow tails as rudders to steer in the water. Muskrats also have webbed hind feet. They use their feet to propel them when they swim.

Spider Monkeys

Spider monkeys live high up in the trees. They chatter to the animals below and toss nuts to them. Spider monkeys are the star acrobats of the jungle—all because of their tails. They wrap their tails around branches and swing from tree to tree. Now and then, as they dangle in mid-air, spider monkeys stop to pick a banana. Since swinging with a partner is a great way to play around, two spider monkeys twine their tails together and rock to and fro.

Peacocks

As the male peacock struts around the forests of India and Sri Lanka, he drags long tail feathers behind him. But when he wants to impress a lady peacock, he spreads his tail feathers out into a huge fan. The tail looks like a rainbow with eye–spots. The male peacock wants the lady peacock to think he is the best peacock in the whole forest.

Foxes

When the clever fox is ready to snooze, it wraps its thick, furry tail around its body. The tail covers the fox's face and makes a warm and furry eyeshade. But the fox is sleepy only in the day. At night, when the fox trots quickly through the woods searching for food, it carries its tail straight out and uses it as a guide through the darkness.

Animal Hiders

Imagine if people had spots or stripes. Then we could blend
into the shadows. Or, what if our color changed with the
seasons. We would be brown like the earth in the summer
and white like the snow in winter. We could hide whenever
we wanted. Some animals are lucky in this way. They have dark
and light markings. For others, their colors change with the
seasons or the time of day. All of these animals can safely hide
wherever they live. This is called *camouflage*.

Leopards

As it crawls up the branches of a tree and crouches under the leaves, a leopard cannot be seen. It has black and brown spots that look like paw prints covering its yellow coat. From far away, these special markings appear to be the sun shining through the tiny leaves on the tree. The rest of the forest life does not know that a leopard is up in the tree eating dinner, sleeping safely, or keeping an alert eye on all the forest activity.

Chameleons

The chameleon is a lizard of <u>many</u> colors that keep changing. It can hide whenever it wants. With bulging eyes and a tail that grabs onto branches, the chameleon shoots out its tongue to catch insects. During the day, when the chameleon crawls up trees, its color is green. At night, when the chameleon creeps over the bare earth, it is tan with yellow spots. When it is frightened, the chameleon has brown patches. When it is not threatened, the chameleon is green with dark patches.

Snowshoe Hares

The snowshoe hare's habits—not just the color of its fur—change with the seasons. In the summer, when the earth is brown, the snowshoe hare has brown fur. Since it cannot easily be seen against the earth, the snowshoe hare lives in the hills and eats leaves. In the winter, when snow covers the earth, the snowshoe hare turns white. Then it floats on logs in the swamps and eats tree bark.

Zebras

Herds of wild zebras live on the African plains. Zebras are very shy animals. They stay with their herds. Luckily, the black and white stripes make it easy for zebras to hide in the tall blades of grass that grow on the plains. From a distance, it is hard to see where the grass ends and the zebras begin. Closer up, it is easier to spot the animals. But this does not worry the powerful zebras who quickly gallop away at the first sign of danger.

Giraffes

Giraffes are the tallest animals in the world. They are three times taller than full-grown people. With their long necks, giraffes can poke their heads high up into the trees and feast on the leaves at the top. Giraffes do not worry about other animals seeing them. Their brown and white markings blend perfectly with the branches and shadows of the trees.

Tricksters, Acrobats, and Snoops

Magicians in painted circus tents are not the only tricksters. Trapeze artists and tightrope walkers are not the only acrobats. And clowns poking their red noses into other people's business are not the only snoops. Sometimes the animal kingdom is like a circus with many of the greatest gags performed by animals. In the ocean, there are vanishing acts. In the trees, there are ventriloquists. And in the woods, hungry snoops can be found.

Elephants

The elephant lumbers through the forests of Africa and Asia.
Two thick teeth called tusks curve out of its mouth. A long
snout called a trunk hangs from its face. Some elephants weigh
10,000 pounds—others weigh even more. The elephant doesn't
need help to wash its huge body. It just sucks water into its trunk
and sprays it all over its back. This is quite a trunk-twirling act!
The elephant also carries logs, pulls down branches, and picks
up food with its incredible trunk.

Parrots

"Tst! Tst!" cries the parrot, the feathered ventriloquist of the jungle. It fools other animals into thinking it's a spider monkey, swinging above, getting ready to throw a nut to the ground. *"Oooooooh,"* it cries again. This time it's pretending to be the wind racing by so the other animals think a storm is brewing. The parrot loves to confuse its neighbors, causing them to scatter away. And while they are gone it helps itself to all the leftover seeds and fruits it can find.

Skunks

If a skunk comes across an animal that is a bit too nosey, it does a handstand and walks away on its front feet. Some skunks even click their teeth at the same time. This is a warning to others that they are trespassing on the skunk's territory. If the busybody doesn't watch out, the skunk sprays a nasty smelling liquid. If the animal is too slow getting away, it will smell terrible for quite some time. The reason skunks warn their intruders before spraying is that they dislike the smell, too.

Sea Otters

There is nothing more irritating for the sea otter than diving to the ocean floor and surfacing with a clam that cannot be opened. That is why the sea otter also finds a rock while it is underwater. Since it is hard to carry a clam and a rock and swim at the same time, the clever otter tucks the clam under its arm until it gets to the surface of the ocean. Floating on its back, the otter balances the rock on its chest and bangs the clam against the rock until the shell opens. Some sea otters have favorite rocks that they keep under their arms all the time.

River Otters

Up a slippery hill climbs the river otter. It stands in line behind the other otters awaiting its turn to slide down the icy slope. When the chance comes, the otter pushes off with its hind legs and slides down the ice on its tummy. Sometimes, an otter races down the hill at a speed of 17 miles per hour.

The river otter is also an expert swimmer. It can dive down 60 feet and swim in the water under the ice for a quarter of a mile. The otter does this by breathing in oxygen from air bubbles trapped in pockets beneath the ice.

Wolverines

The real animal bandit of North America seems to be the wolverine. When the weak-sighted wolverine hears a woodsman, it follows him to his cabin. Then the wily wolverine hides in the trees outside. When the woodsman leaves again, the wolverine runs inside the cabin and makes a huge mess as it searches and steals all the food. On days when the wolverine doesn't find a woodsman, it simply finds a woodsman's traps and grabs everything caught inside.

Octopuses

The prowling, hungry moray eel makes life in the ocean rough for most sea animals. But the intelligent octopus has found a way to outsmart the eel. The octopus sprays a kind of brown ink into the eel's face. The ink creates a dark screen that blinds the eel and blocks its sense of smell. Now the octopus has a chance to escape any danger. But it must swim away quickly because the ink will soon disappear.

Armadillos

In Spanish, armadillo means "a little armored thing," and most of this animal's body and head is like armor. The armor is made of thorny shields. But armadillos are not always "little things." While some are only five inches long, others are as long as five feet.

When an armadillo sees a scary-looking animal, like a coyote, it rolls itself into a tight ball. The coyote bounces around this roly-poly ball trying to get it to unwind. But the armadillo doesn't mind being bounced because its shields prevent it from getting hurt.

Animal Construction Workers

Have you ever watched construction workers and thought, "Wow, their work looks like fun"? They have all kinds of shiny tools and sit high up in the air on beams. Well, certain animals are skilled construction workers, too. For example, nests, dams, and burrows are all homes built by animals.

Storks

High over European villages, white storks fly carrying sticks in their beaks. Down on the rooftops they settle to build their nests, which look like blankets of branches. Other storks flock around them bending back their heads and clapping their beaks together to make rattling sounds. "Welcome to the neighborhood!" they seem to say. Storks build their homes on neighboring rooftops so they can be near each other.

Chipmunks

Deep under the ground, the chipmunk is busily digging a home. Carefully, it plans a home that is like a three-room apartment. The first room is carpeted with thick green moss for a comfortable bed. Then, the chipmunk makes a room with double walls where the family can cuddle together on crisp winter days. Finally, the chipmunk digs a storeroom filled with enough seeds to last the winter. The chipmunk is a clever planner and does not waste a bit of space.

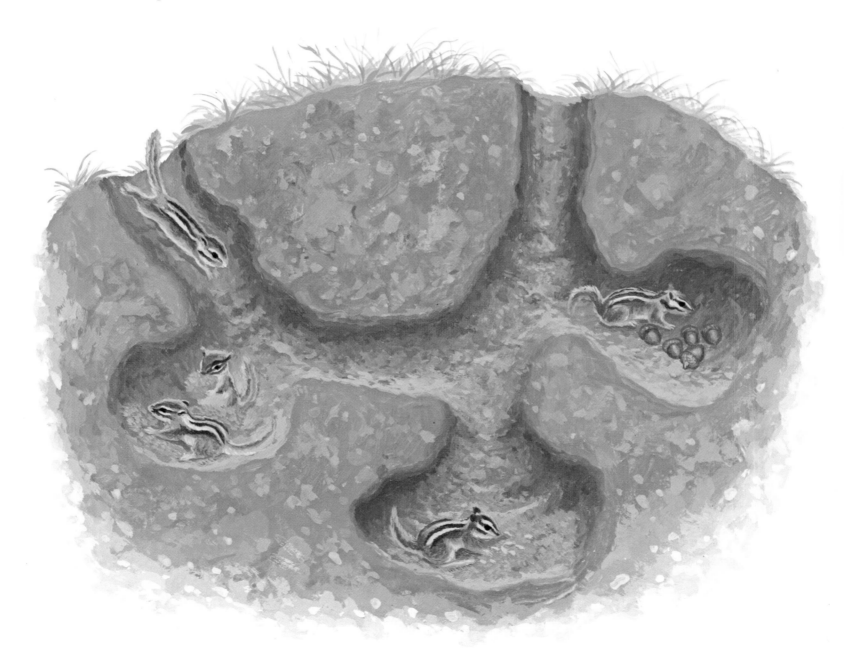

Wolves

Wolves often travel in packs. In the winter, they climb bluffs
and sleep on the ice. In the spring, they settle down and build
dens for the new-born wolves. Each female wolf digs a long
tunnel and scoops out a large room at the end of the den,
with smaller rooms off to the sides. She builds passages
leading from the smaller rooms to the outside. She covers the
entryway to the tunnel with rocks so that the babies can safely
look out. After two months, the babies are able to play outside.
When they have learned how to hunt, the wolf pack starts
traveling again.

Beavers

When a male and a female beaver are about two years old, they scamper downstream to build a dam together. First they construct a dam to slow down the rushing flow of the stream. They put sticks between the stones in the water and set logs on top of the sticks. Soon, there are so many logs that they tower in the air. If there are a few gaps between the logs, the beavers plug them up with rocks and grass and anything else they can find.

Now, the beavers are ready to build their lodge behind the dam on the riverbank. The lodge is going to be their home. They fasten twigs in the pond mud, and pile sticks on top of the twigs, until the structure is shaped like a little wigwam. To glue everything together, they plaster mud over the structure. Next the beavers build a few rooms. They jump into the pond and cut out a doorway and scoop out a room or two. Since they might want to take a trip into the forest, they dig a long tunnel from their home to the trees. The beavers have made a safe and sturdy home.

Family Folk

Think how much fun family life can be. Swimming and picnicking on hot summer days. Sledding and ice skating on crisp winter days. Spending time listening to stories about how things were when your parents were your age. Sometimes it seems that animal families enjoy family life, too. There are animal families that travel through the forests in small bands and camp out each night. Other families journey together over snow-capped mountains. Some families help build each other's homes. Yes, animal families seem happy being together, too.

Caribou

Every spring hundreds of caribou families gather together to begin a 700-mile march from their home in Alaska to the Arctic. This march is called a *migration*. In each caribou family there is a father, called a buck, several mothers, called cows, and their babies, called calves. The caribou plan their march so that each animal knows its place. The mothers are up front leading the group. The fathers guard the back and chase away intruders. The calves trot cozily in the middle.

Seals

Alaskan fur seals live in very large families—but only during the summer. Each May, the male, called a bull, swims to the Pribilof Islands near Alaska. Once ashore, he claims a piece of the beach and waits for the arrival of the female seals. When they come, it is his job to win over at least 40 female seals to his part of the beach. All around him, other bulls are doing the same thing.

Many of the arriving females give birth to babies they have been carrying throughout the long winter. The parents spend the summer teaching the baby seals how to swim and catch fish. After four months, the babies are able to live in the water alone. Now the seals leave the island and go south for the winter.

Penguins

Like people huddled together in a crowded train, emperor penguins of Antarctica stand close together in their cramped communities. They don't seem to mind this and they enjoy standing. After a female penguin lays her egg, she swims out to sea to dine on shrimp. It is the male penguin who stays at home and keeps the egg warm by balancing it on his feet. During this time, he may not eat at all. A month after the baby hatches, the female returns to feed it and relieves the male penguin of his duties. Now he can go swimming and catch up on his eating.

Gorillas

Every day these gentle animals wander through the African forest in small families called bands. Although people believe gorillas are fierce animals, they never attack unless they are bullied. Even then, the male gorilla usually first beats his fists against his chest and roars, hoping to scare away the intruder. In most gorilla families there is a male, two females, and their babies. Each night the band picks a different tree in the forest and builds a platform in the branches. Everyone sleeps there except the male gorilla. He sits on the ground and keeps a sleepy watch over his family.

Lions

When a female lion is ready to have babies, she rests in a thicket until her babies are born. She leaves behind the rest of her family, called a pride, which consists of a male lion, several lionesses, and their cubs. When the lioness's babies are born they will be almost helpless. They will need special care and attention from their mother until they are about ten weeks old. After that time, the lioness and her cubs rejoin the rest of the pride as they wander over the hot African plains.

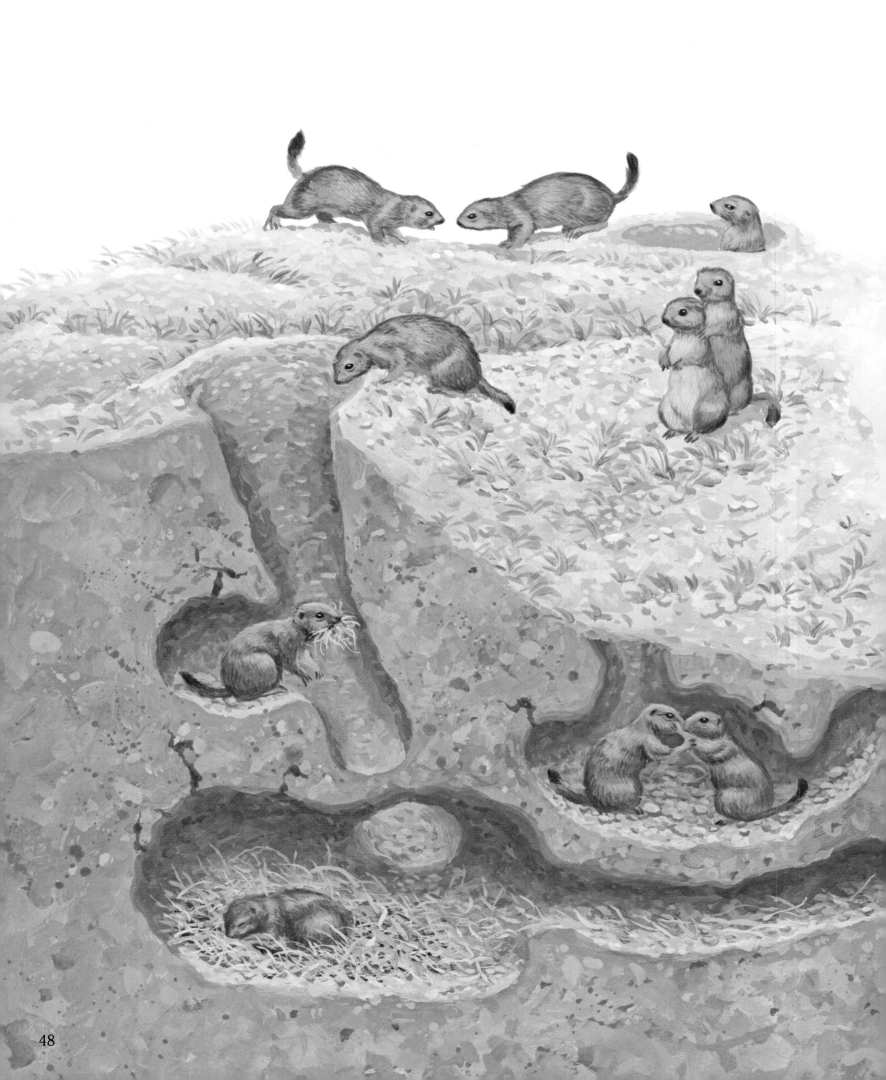

Prairie Dogs

"Chirp, chirp," cries a prairie dog to alert others of danger. His brothers might scamper out of their burrows to see what's wrong. His sisters might poke their heads out of a listening post to see if their brothers are arguing with an intruder. Prairie dogs are very protective and will not let a stranger onto their land.

These little animals are not really dogs but are in the same family as squirrels. The prairie dog gets its name from its warning call, which sounds like a dog's loud barking. A prairie dog family often has one father, four mothers, and several children. The family is called a *coterie*. The family members are very close. They groom each other, hug and kiss, and play together. They live in large underground towns, which they divide into areas called territories. Each coterie stays in its own territory. The territory has many burrows for the prairie dogs to live in.

A burrow usually has two entrances—one is for quick escapes. A burrow also has a tunnel with a listening post near the top, a room to sleep in, and a dryroom built in a special way so that rain cannot drip inside. But even if a storm comes, prairie dogs don't worry too much about their homes getting soggy. They have packed mounds of dirt around the entrances so the rain will slide back down the front and not drain into their tunnels.

Winter Snoozers and Deep Sleepers

In the fall, when the wind whistles a chilling tune through the bushes, some warm-blooded animals, like foxes, don't worry about the cold because they grow thick coats of fur. Other warm-blooded animals, like bears, don't grow such luxurious coats. For these animals, it is time to find a comfortable place to sleep through the cold weather. On a warm winter day, they might wake up for an hour or two and then fall back to sleep again. But there are some animals that sleep soundly all winter long. They are cold-blooded animals, like lizards. They do not feel cold or hungry. This kind of deep sleep is called *hibernation*.

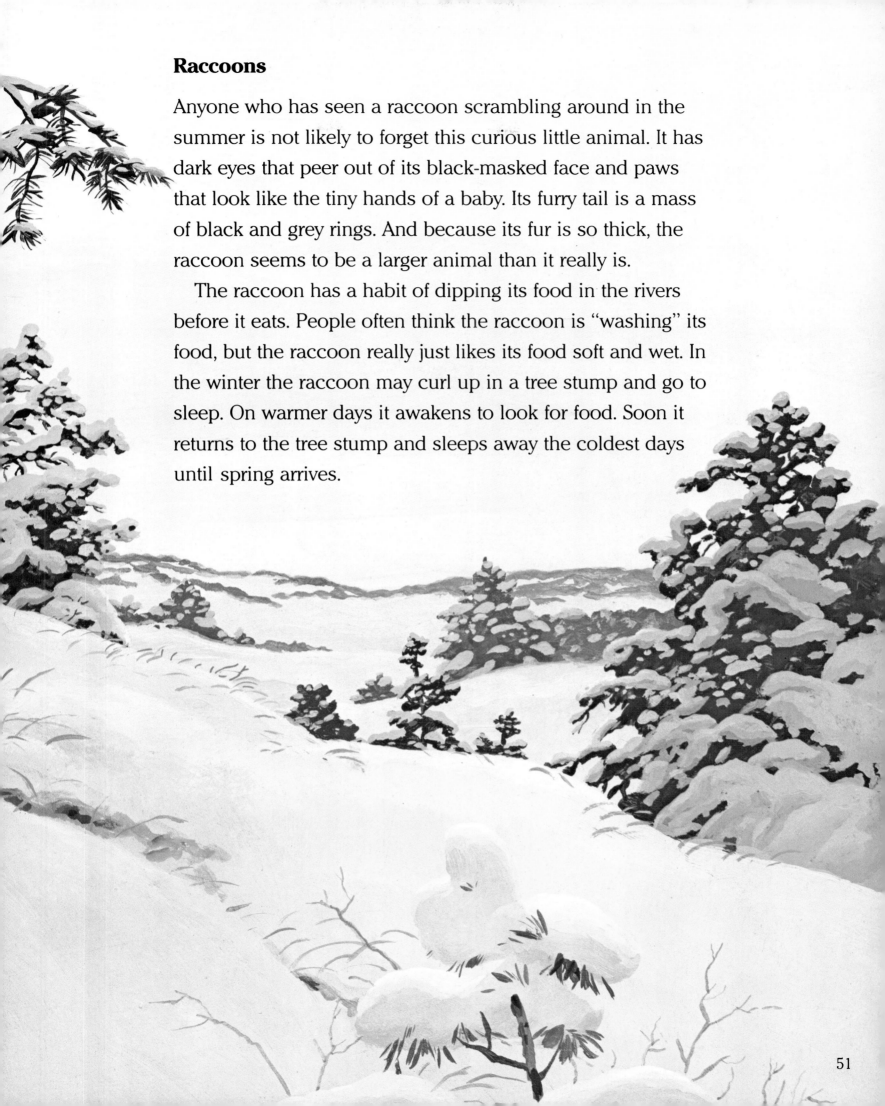

Raccoons

Anyone who has seen a raccoon scrambling around in the summer is not likely to forget this curious little animal. It has dark eyes that peer out of its black-masked face and paws that look like the tiny hands of a baby. Its furry tail is a mass of black and grey rings. And because its fur is so thick, the raccoon seems to be a larger animal than it really is.

The raccoon has a habit of dipping its food in the rivers before it eats. People often think the raccoon is "washing" its food, but the raccoon really just likes its food soft and wet. In the winter the raccoon may curl up in a tree stump and go to sleep. On warmer days it awakens to look for food. Soon it returns to the tree stump and sleeps away the coldest days until spring arrives.

Fox Squirrels

Chilly autumn air turns the fox squirrel into a master builder. To prepare a winter home, the fox squirrel scurries up a tree, sits on a chunky branch, and begins to bite off twigs. Then it weaves them into a nest that looks like a ball. Next the fox squirrel slaps wet leaves on the nest to make it stronger. But the wind can still slip through the nest, so the clever fox squirrel builds a second wall under the first. This traps the cold air inside the space between the two walls. Now, when the fox squirrel climbs inside, its body heat will warm the nest and make it nice and cozy. Another fox squirrel might be invited to sleep over, but usually a fox squirrel likes to nap alone.

Bears

For people, sleep might be a time of rest from all the activity of the day. For a female black bear, winter sleep is a time to have babies. She prepares for her sleep, or hibernation, by eating so much food that she becomes very fat. Then she finds a den or hollow nest to protect her from the harsh weather while she sleeps away the winter. While the mother bear snoozes, she gives birth to two or three babies, called cubs. The babies weigh only a half to one pound at birth. After one month, the cubs have soft, fuzzy brown fur all over their bodies and are able to open their eyes. When spring comes, the mother bear climbs out of her den with her brand new family.

Turtles

Even though there are a lot of different turtles—some big and some very small—one thing is true for all of them. Turtles are the only reptiles that have shells to protect them from harm.

During the spring and summer, a turtle plods along in the water and on land. But as soon as cold winds blow, it digs a hole in wet mud or soft earth. There the turtle falls into a very deep sleep—so deep that it seems as if it isn't breathing! This means the turtle is hibernating. When winter has gone, the turtle wakes up and begins plodding around once more.

Toads

When the first spring rain arrives, thousands of toads come out
of the earth where they have been hibernating all winter. They
leap in all directions—in the shallow water, on the banks, in
the grass by the river's edge, on the rocks. There are all kinds of
toads—graceful, wobbly, calm, grouchy, short, fat, and scrawny
ones. When male toads want to find mates, they croak songs
to attract females. Soon after the female toads are attracted,
they lay eggs in a pool of water. Then all the toads scatter into
the countryside to search for food.

Animals with Helpers

Have you ever wondered why two people who seem very different are such good friends? They go everywhere together, laugh together, and help each other whenever they can. Animals seem to be like this, too. Some animals are good buddies with animals that are just like them. Other animals are buddies with animals that are quite different. These animal partners clean, feed, and take good care of each other.

Rhinoceroses

The rhinoceros is a fierce animal with no hair, one horn, and very poor eyesight. It stomps through the woods of Africa, India, and Asia. If a rhinoceros is grumpy, it attacks anything that moves. Its temper frightens most animals, except for oxpeckers—small birds who are the rhino's faithful companions. They sit and eat ticks and insects off the rhino's back. These birds also keep watch for any sign of danger. If something approaches, the oxpecker's squawking alerts the rhino. It may have poor eyesight, but a rhino's hearing is very sharp.

Alligators

When the alligator hisses, the swamp animals tremble. When it opens its toothy jaws, most animals run for their lives. But there are some brave little birds who know that tasty food is stuck between the alligator's teeth. So the spur-winged plover flies into the alligator's mouth and nibbles at the food. The alligator doesn't mind the pecking because its teeth are getting cleaned. But the little birds know that too much bravery can be foolish—especially when they are dealing with an alligator. Since an alligator is not very smart, it might forget that the birds are in its mouth and clamp its teeth together. So the birds keep their eyes open and, as soon as they have finished eating, they carefully fly backwards out of the alligator's mouth.

Dolphins

Up and down and in and out of the ocean dart the dolphins. They jump out of the water to catch a breath of air and then return to their swimming. But a new-born dolphin cannot leap yet, so its mother has to help it. She puts her snout under her baby and lifts it into the air with her flipper. Since she is busy watching the baby, she can't watch out for sharks. So a female dolphin friend, called an auntie, swims by her side and keeps a lookout for any sign of deadly shark fins.

Hippopotamuses

All day long herds of hippopotamuses slowly wade in rivers. They look like huge rocks with their stubby legs, small bulging eyes, and four-ton bodies. Each herd stands in a circle. The males always stay on the edges, and the females and their babies stay in the middle. During the day hippopotamuses swim, dig for roots, and walk on the river bottom.

At night, each hippo leaves the herd to search for food on land. Since the babies are too small to travel alone, they must stay in the water with someone watching over them. It must be a female because no male will enter the middle of the circle. Female hippos with no babies of their own mind the youngsters until their mothers return.

Since hippos are underwater so much, algae collects on their skin. Little fish eat the algae on the hippo's leathery skin, so the hippos get a cleaning at the same time.